Illustrations by Monica Wyrick
Layout and design by Diane Florence

ISBN
1889636606

Library of Congress Number
2003113769

10 9 8 7 6 5 4 3 2 1
Printed in the United States

P.O. Box 115 • Chapin, SC 29036
(800) 209-9774 • (803) 345-1070 • Fax (803) 345-0888
yl@sc.rr.com www.youthlight.com

This book is dedicated to my brother
who passed from this life at the age of 41 on November 30, 2001.
He was a free-spirited individual who loved nature
and on his trail rides enjoyed the freedom it had to offer.
My brother had a dog named "Nakoma."
In these stories, Nakoma is the name of Dakota's brother.
Lesson 5 entitled "Dakota Loses His Best Friend"
was written in memory of my brother.

To my brother and friend, Doug Cooke.
You will be remembered forever!

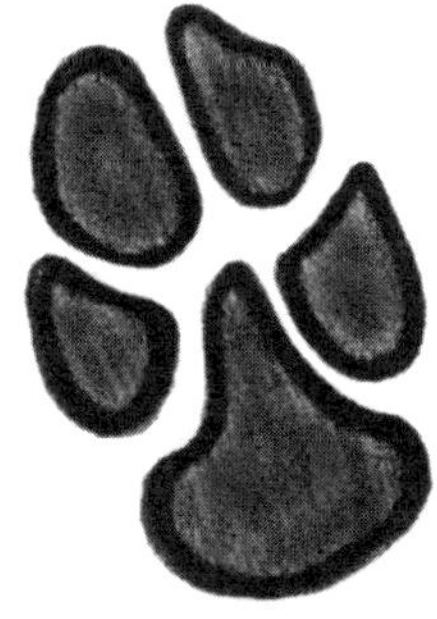

Table of Contents

Acknowledgements

Thanks to Sandy Ragona, Guidance Counselor, and her students at Kennedy Elementary School in Dubuque, Iowa for pilot-testing this program. They provided many helpful suggestions. I enjoyed all the comments from the students and took them into consideration when writing my final draft. In addition, I want to thank Marcy Baumgartner, counselor intern from the University of Wisconsin for her assistance in presenting the stories of Dakota with children in Kennedy Elementary.

I also want to thank Diane Senn, Guidance Counselor at Crowder Creek Elementary in Rock Hill, South Carolina for pilot testing the program. Her encouraging and insightful comments helped me considerably in completing this program.

Thanks to Calvin Orion Bowman (age 8) for helping me think of names for my animal characters and for helping me test some of the activities.

I also acknowledge my husband Bob, my mentor and life-long friend. If it wasn't for his encouragement, guidance and support this book may have never been written. Thank you for believing in me and for helping me bring the character, Dakota, to life.

I especially thank God for His guidance and direction throughout my life. I thank Him for allowing me the opportunity to share the gifts He has given me with others.

Introduction

Why a book about a wolf? I have had a fascination with wolves as long as I can remember. Wolves are such special creatures and can teach us so much about working together, loyalty, nurturing, social skills, persistence and many other valuable life lessons. I have two main reasons for writing a book about a wolf.

First, I know what it feels like to have a bad reputation. When I was a student in elementary school I was a low achiever and had behavior problems because I did not feel successful or worthwhile. I earned a reputation of being a "bad" kid and not liked very much by my teachers. In fourth grade I became truant so much that I had to repeat the grade over. I felt like no one understood what I was going through.

In the same way, wolves are misunderstood. They have gained a reputation through folklore as being "mean" or "bad". Unfortunately, many of our kids have been labeled "bad kids". However, once society started taking an interest in studying wolf behavior, they learned how valuable the wolves were to the balance of nature and that actual cases of a wolf attack were far and few unlike what they had heard. Likewise, when educators take an interest in studying "difficult" kids they too discover that these kids are a valuable resource to our schools and communities and that actual reported cases of a violent act are far and few. What these kids need are caring adults who believe in their potential and are invested in helping them to change their reputation. These caring adults can help students learn a lot from wolf pack behavior since the pack:

- maintains discipline among its members.
- provides support for one another.
- teaches life skills to all the young.
- supplies basic needs.
- provides protection and safety.
- works together as a team to get things done.

The second reason for writing this book is because the wolf Pack can teach our children valuable life skills such as character, coping, compassion and group decision making/problem solving. Many children are more likely to listen to the advice of their peers than an adult. For that reason they need to learn appropriate problem-solving skills and have opportunities for practicing these skills. This book is designed to do just that. Dakota is a wolf who shares different challenges that he and other animals have faced in the wild. Children are encouraged to relate the lessons in these stories to their own situations.

How To Use This Book

Before starting, make as many copies as needed of the paw-print on page 7. You may want each child in the small group to have one or have one per group. Next divide the class into small groups (packs) of four to five students and give a paw-print page to each group. Ask each group to select a name for their pack. One way to do this is to have each student write a suggested name on a piece of paper without telling the other students the name they chose. Then read each suggested name and have the pack vote on which name they will use. For younger students you may want to give them a list of names and have them pick the one they most like. Once a name is selected have a member of each pack to cut out the paw-prints and write their pack's name on each of them. These paw-prints can be kept by the students and/or displayed on their desk, a bulletin board, hall display or somewhere in the classroom.

(Variation: Each student could choose a wolf name to put on their own paw-print and color them if they choose to.)

When selecting packs, if possible, include a good cross section of students and do not end up with packs consisting of students who are all leaders, attention seekers, shy, talkative, etc. After reading the beginning of each story Dakota will share a challenging situation. Read until you see where it says "Paws Time" marked with a paw print. This is where you pause the story and have the students get into their wolf packs. Ask students to discuss answers to the questions provided. Then students brainstorm possible solutions to the situation in Dakota's story. After each pack shares their ideas, you resume the story where Dakota tells the children how the situation in the story was resolved.

(Variation: Each pack can attach a wooden stick or plastic straw to their paw-print. When the pack is ready to share their ideas, students can hold up their paw-prints to let you know that they are ready to share.)

This program can be presented to children during any part of the school day. Since the stories promote character building, problem solving, conflict resolution, teamwork, conservation, and critical thinking they will fit into most academic content areas. In particular, its teachings align well with the goals of developmental guidance, social studies, science, English, and health education. Each story with the discussion questions will require about twenty minutes to complete. The optional role plays and activity sheets will add more time to each lesson. Or as a review, they can be completed by students at a later time.

At any point in this program, I encourage you to share with your students the section called "Wolf Facts" in Appendix A. The information is explained in a way that young students can understand. It tells about the many challenges that wolves have faced throughout the years. It also helps to educate students on what the term "endangered" means, how wolves have had a "bad rep" over the years and what efforts have been taken to disprove their bad reputation and help them to survive. Students are invited to learn more about wolf recovery programs through websites and other sources of information found in Appendix C.

You may want to begin the program with The Maligned Wolf story (found in Appendix B). This story gives the wolf's account of what happened in the story of Little Red Riding Hood that was written in the late 1600s. This could be a good way to introduce Dakota and talk to the students about how there are always two sides to a story.

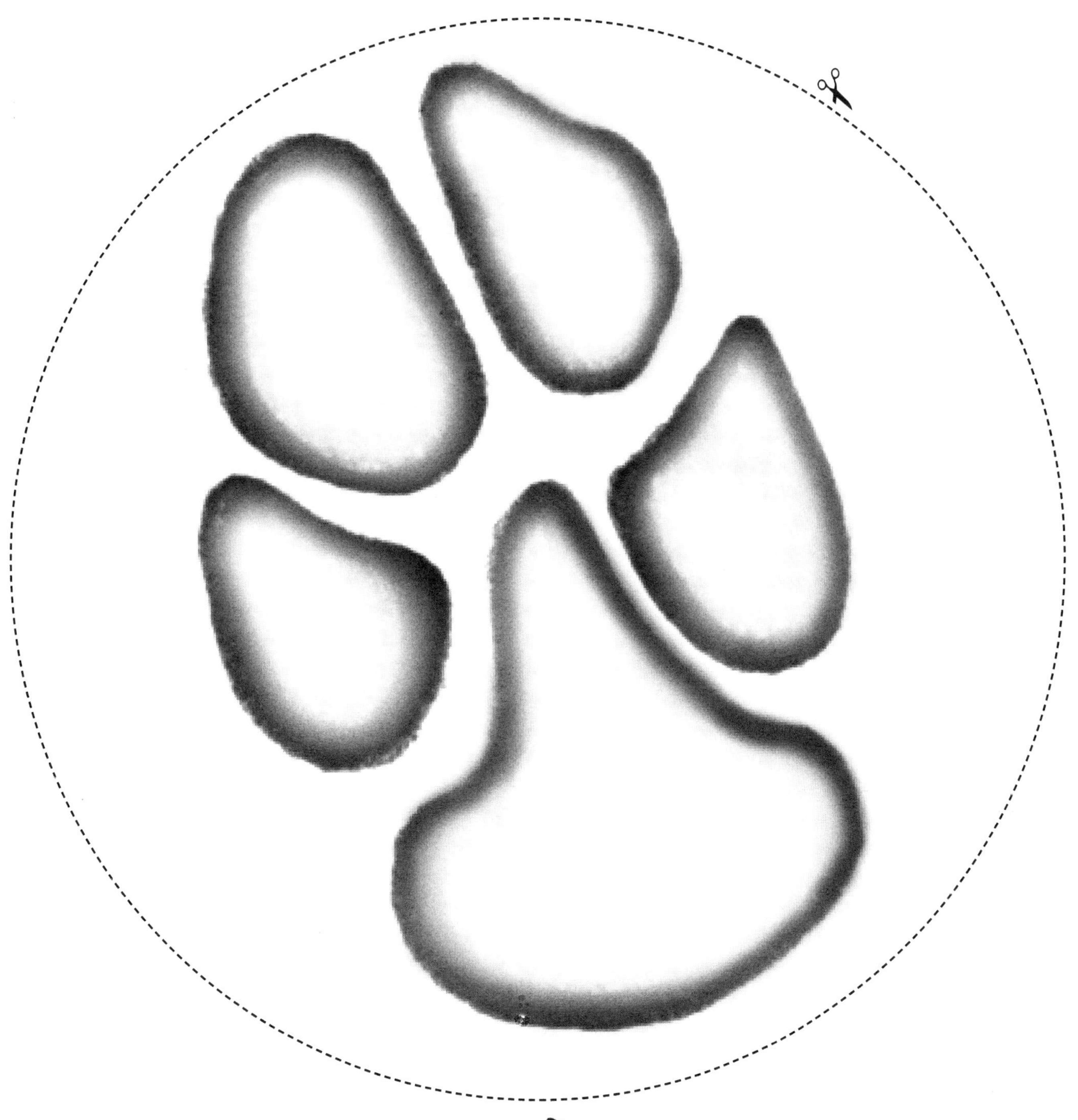

Meet Dakota, the Friendly Wolf

Hi, my name is Dakota. Let me tell you a little about myself. I am a wolf. No, I'm not bad or mean like the stories you might have heard about when you were younger. I'm sure many of you heard stories like, "Little Red Riding Hood," "The Three Little Pigs," or "The Boy Who Cried Wolf." Unfortunately, these stories have made us look like mean, vicious killers. Well those stories are not true they are just ancient fables. These days it is hard to find any stories about wolves that are positive. Many of you know what a reputation (rep) is. Well, I want to change our reputation and at the same time share some of my life experiences with you.

I want to share with you some of the adventures I have had growing up. After hearing about each of my adventures, there will be a time when I need your help to think of different ways I could handle a situation. When you hear the words "Paws Time," that means to meet together in your small groups called, wolf packs, to think together of answers to questions about the story. Then, someone will share your pack's ideas with the rest of the class. After all packs have a turn to share their ideas, you will hear the rest of my story and what I decided to do. Then you will have a chance to share a time in your own life that was similar to my story and how you handled it.

Dakota Outsmarts the Foxes

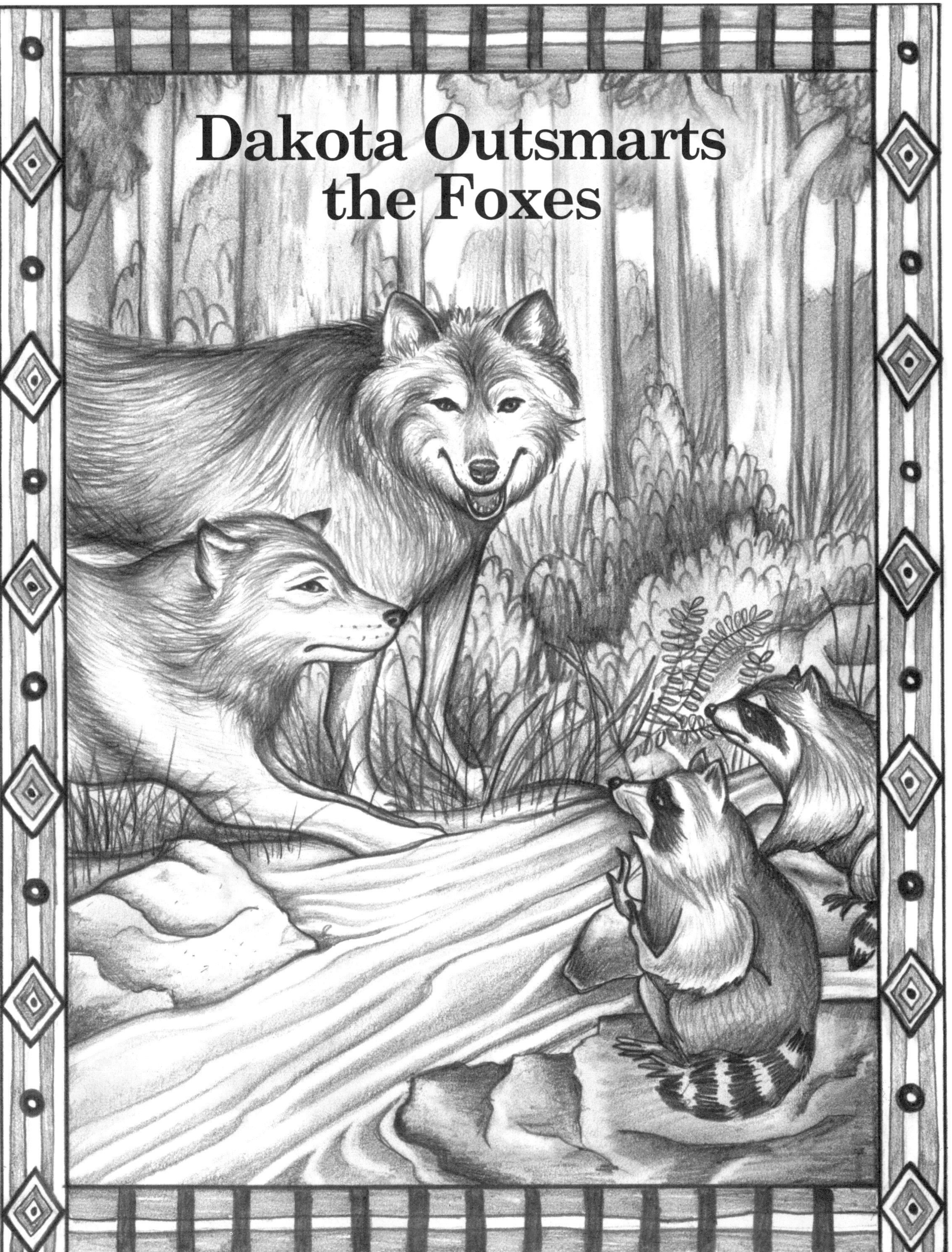

When I was a pup I learned about the many dangers in the forest and how other animals would say terrible things about us and spread rumors that all of us wolves were mean. I didn't like being called names such as "The Big Bad Wolf" or "Killer" and I was determined that I would prove to the other animals that wolves are not all bad or mean. Let me tell you a story about a time when that happened.

One day while out playing by the brook with my brother, Nakoma, two young raccoons came running across the large rocks in the stream. Once they spotted us they came to a sudden halt.

Nakoma and I decided to go meet them. Before we could get close they started yelling, "Stay away! We heard about you. The foxes told us about your kind."

I replied, "But, we just want to be...," they ran off through the bushes before I could finish my sentence.

Nakoma and I felt very hurt and rejected. Without even knowing anything about us and by just hearing rumors from some foxes they judged us as being "bad." So we tried to ignore all this and find some other animals to play with.

Soon we spotted a new animal in our forest, a cougar. "Surely she would play with us," I said to my brother.

But as we got closer the cougar looked the other way and mumbled, loud enough that we could hear, "Wolves..., I know all about them."

Nakoma started to get angry but couldn't think of a way to stop the rumors so he just decided to go home and play with some other wolves from our pack.

"Don't you care what other animals think of us?" I said to Nakoma. I tried to think of ways I could show these foxes and other animals that we were not bad or mean like they had heard. But, how could I show them that we were not mean or bad wolves?

Paws Time

Ask students to meet in their "wolf packs" and discuss their answers to the following questions.

- *What did the cougar think of Dakota and his brother?*
- *How did the rumor start and then spread?*
- *How could Dakota convince the foxes that he was a nice and caring wolf?*

Next, have each wolf pack share their ideas with the entire class. Then continue the story by saying, Let's find out what Dakota decided to do.

I decided that I couldn't make the foxes believe that I was nice just by telling them, so I would show them by giving a friendship gift. I tried to think of something they might like. Then I remembered how much they liked berries. I decided to take a basket of wild, juicy berries that I had carefully picked and brought over to the foxes den.

One of the foxes saw me leave the basket and told the others, "Hey remember those wolves we heard about, look what one of them brought us?" "Maybe they're not so mean after all.

The next time I saw the foxes playing in the woods they didn't say anything to me. Eventually one of them thanked me for my gift. But even if he hadn't thank me, I felt proud that I could outsmart those foxes and do something kind for them that they would never expect me to do.

Later, a new rumor started going around our forest. The animals were now saying that wolves are not all "Bad" like some of the stories they heard. I even heard that some foxes were telling other animals that we wolves were pretty smart!

Follow-up Questions

- If someone told other people that you were mean or bad, how could you show them that the rumor was not true?
- If you heard someone talking about how bad another student was, what could you do or say?

Follow-up Role-Play

Role-play the following situation and then answer the questions that follow.

Characters

- Three students spreading rumors
- A new student to the school who wants to make friends
- The student who the rumors are about who tries to make friends with the new student

Situation

Three children are at recess and begin talking to each other. One of them starts saying mean things about another student they barely know. The other two join in on the gossip. A new student to the school overhears the children talking and learns that this other student they are talking about is very mean. The student who they are talking about walks over to introduce him/herself to the new student and the new student says, "I heard about you and I'm not allowed to hang around kids like you." The student becomes very angry but knows if he/she says anything mean it will just prove to the new student that the rumor is true. Stop the skit.

Discuss:

- What was happening in the skit?
- How did the rumor start?
- What do you think was the reason the new student listened to the rumor?
- How do you think that student felt after finding out the new student heard that he/she was mean?
- What do you think the student should do in this situation?

Optional Activity:

Have students act out these responses.

ACTIVITY: 1

See what happens when a rumor goes
from one animal to another in this maze.

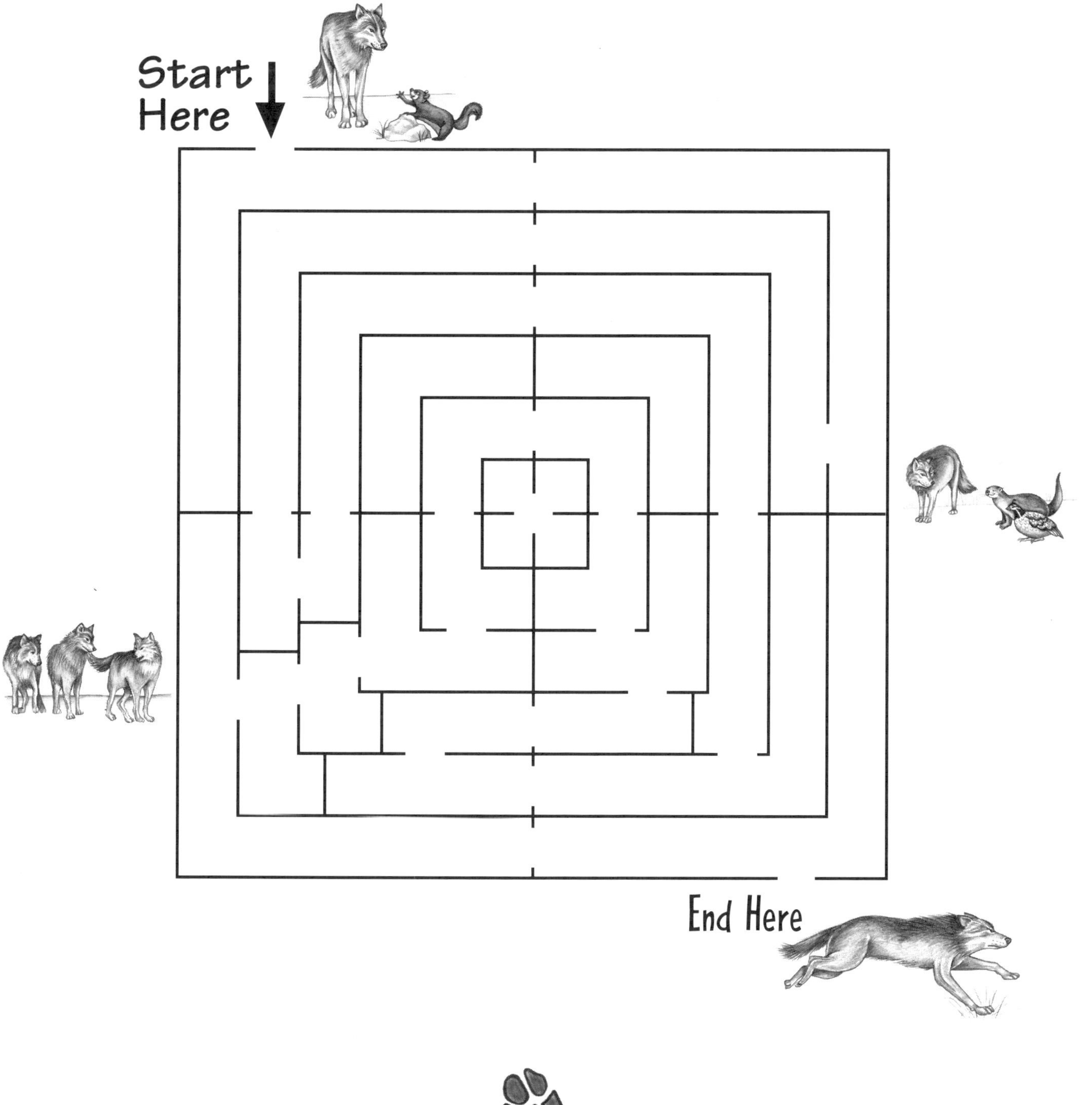

Start Here

End Here

Dakota Faces Bobbie
the Bully Bobcat

One day I was walking along my favorite stream, I decided to practice jumping from one rock to another without slipping, I was jumping along when all of a sudden, "Ker Splash," my paw missed a rock and I fell in the stream. Soaked, I ran quickly out of the water and shook myself off. I heard a loud laugh from behind me. I turned around and saw "Bobbie" the bobcat, known by other animals as "Bully Bobcat," who picked on other animals in our forest.

Already feeling discouraged I told her, "Your not nice, just leave me alone," but she just kept on teasing me. She stuck her nose up and said, "Your such a 'Klutz' I can jump across the entire stream and not fall. I can even do it with my eyes closed."

Embarrassed I said, "Well, I can too, sometimes." Bobbie starting laughing. Then I got mad and said, "You're just a Bully Bobcat, don't you have anything better to do then go around teasing others?" She just kept following me around and teasing me. I tried ignoring her but that didn't work either. I was running out of ways to keep her off my back!

Paws Time

Ask students to meet in their "wolf packs" and discuss their answers to the following questions.

- *How do you think Dakota felt when Bobbie laughed at him?*
- *What do you think Dakota could say or do to get Bobbie to stop teasing him?*

Next, have each wolf pack share their ideas with the entire class. Then continue the story by saying, Let's find out what Dakota decided to do.

Bobbie snickered and said, "What's wrong, afraid you will fall down again?" I stopped for a minute and thought in my head, why does Bobbie always bully other animals? Then I thought to myself that she only hangs around other animals that she can tease. So I had an idea! Maybe I could do something that she wouldn't expect and invite Bobbie to play a game with me. I was kind of scared of what she would say to me but thought it can't be any worse than what she was saying to me now.

I took a deep breath, looked Bobbie in the face and said, "When you say mean things to me it makes me sad and mad and makes me not want to be around you!" I then nervously asked, "Why not do something fun together instead." Bobbie laughed at me and said, "Why would I want to play with you?"

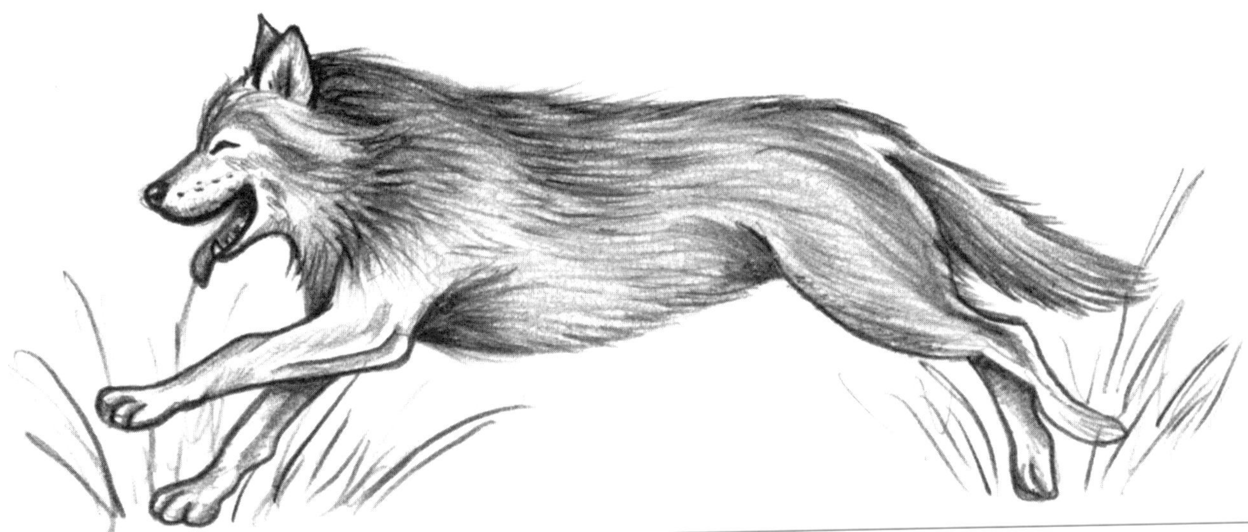

I replied, “Well, I thought you might like to race up Big Rock, the highest point in our forest, unless of course you don’t think you can run that far!” She liked the idea of doing something she knew she was very good at and snickered, “Sure, I’ll race you there.” I knew she would climb faster than I would but I wanted to do something to show her that we could play together.

We discovered that I was better at running and she was better at climbing so we both had things we were good at. After spending more time with Bobbie I found out that she really didn’t like being mean to other animals.

One day Bobbie surprised me and said, “I always wished I could be more like you because you always have friends to play with.” Wow, what a surprise that was! That She would want to be more like Me! Bobbie and I spent many more days together, talking and playing. Other animals noticed her being friendlier and invited her to play with them as well. Soon, instead of calling her “Bobbie the Bully Bobcat” she was called “Bobbie the Friendly Bobcat.”

Follow-up Questions

- Have you ever got real mad at someone who made fun of something you did? What happened?
- Have you ever had someone call you names? If so what did you do?

Follow-up Role-Play

Role-play the following situation and then answer the questions that follow.

Characters

- A student who is showing his/her friends how they can do a trick on their skateboard
- Several other students watching
- A bully who laughs when the student messes up and makes fun of him/her

Situation

A group of kids are playing at a local park. One of the kids decides to show them a trick on the skateboard that he/she has been working on. Another person who is known to be a bully is also standing there and sees him/her trying to do a trick but wiping out instead. The bully says something mean to the kid on the skateboard and starts laughing. The other kids (who are supposed to be the friends of the one on the skateboard) start laughing too. The kid on the skateboard is feeling very embarrassed, hurt and mad. He/she wants to say something mean but his/her friends are all watching. Stop the skit.

Discuss:

- What was happening in the skit?
- How did the person who was laughed at feel? (hurt, mad, embarrassed, belittled, discouraged)
- What do you think was the reason the bully made fun of him/her?
- What do you think was the reason the skateboarder's friends starting laughing?
- What do you think the kid with the skateboard should do in this situation? What about his/her friends?

Optional Activity:

Have students act out these responses.

ACTIVITY: 2

How To Be a Bully Buster

Circle the best response to each of the following situations.

1. You see a fight in the hallway at school.

Cheer on the person you think will win the fight.

Try to break up the fight.

Go find the nearest adult to help.

2. Someone tells you that their going to "get you" after school.

Find a different way home from school and tell your parent(s) later.

Tell a trusted adult that this person threatened to get you after school.

Tell this person that you will be waiting for them with your friends.

3. You keep getting picked on by the same student.

Threaten to beat this person up.

Ask this student if they want to do something fun together.

Try to avoid this student and ignore the teasing.

4. Your friends tease another student and want you to join them.

Tell your friends that what their doing is mean and walk away.

Start teasing the student too so you don't lose your friends.

Don't tease the student but laugh while your friends do.

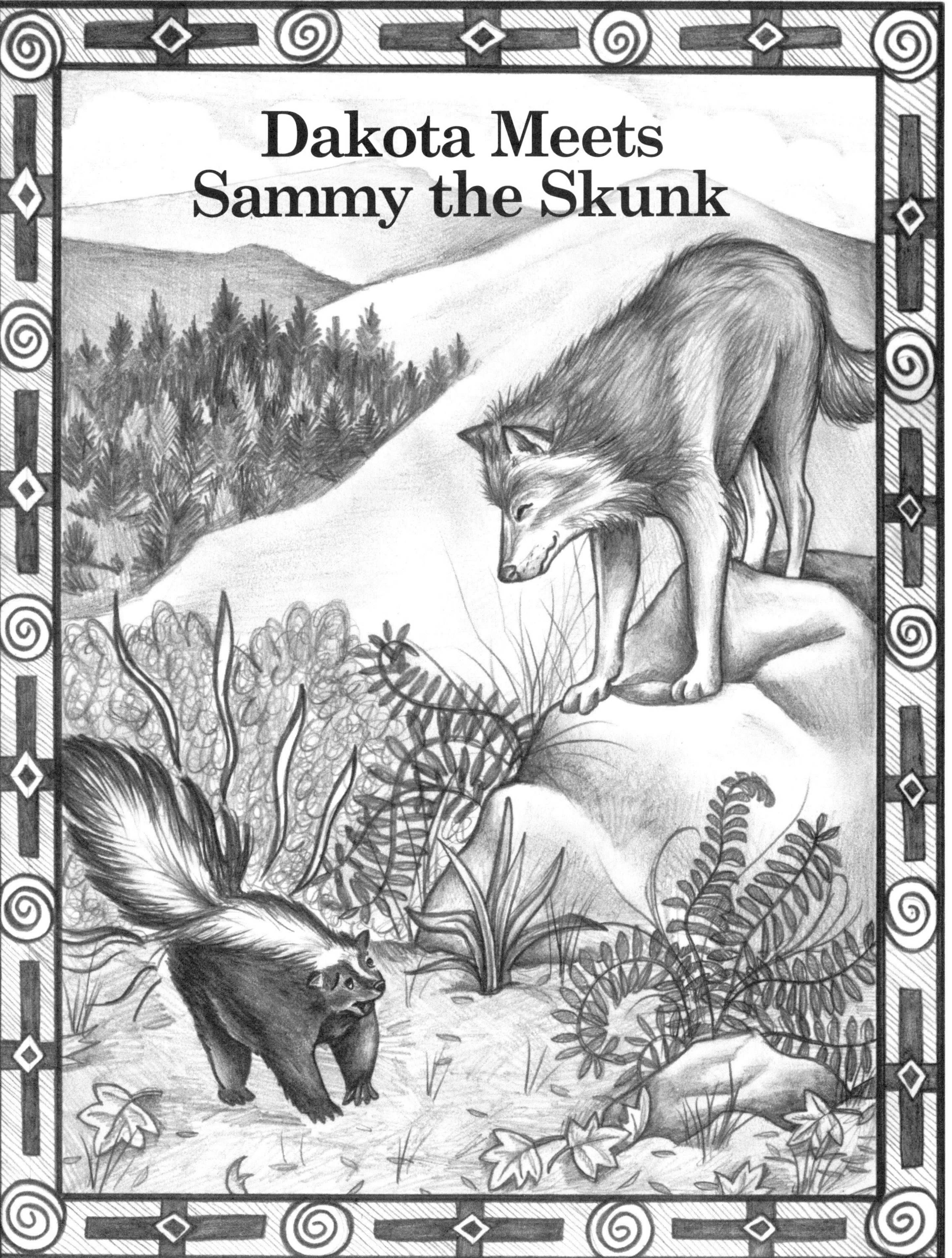
Dakota Meets
Sammy the Skunk

One hot summer day I was enjoying a nice swim in the cool waters of a mountain stream. All of a sudden a terrible odor filled the air. It was so bad I just had to find out where it was coming from so I could get as far away from whatever it was! I got out of the water and shook myself off and looked in every direction. As I looked down, right below the rock I was standing on, I saw a small black and white animal with a very bushy tail that stood straight up in the air. I said; "Hey there, do you know what that terrible smell is?"

The creature very slowly looked up at me and said, "That odor is coming from me, Sammy, and I thought there was a human nearby and got scared and…well…that's what I do to protect myself."

It was difficult standing near Sammy while he talked so I asked him, "Can you stand further away, it's hard to breathe!" When I told him that he looked very sad and said, "You are just like all the other animals I meet." He then slowly slumped away out of sight.

What did he mean when he said, "I was like all the other animals?" I decided to go and ask my dad why skunks smell so bad. My dad laughed and said, "Skunks spray an awful odor to protect themselves from harm just like we use our claws and sharp teeth to protect ourselves." I wondered how I could be a friend with another animal that smelled so bad. I felt bad for Sammy and wanted to find him and say I was sorry for making him go away. But how could I go near him with him smelling so bad?

Paws Time

Ask students to meet in their "wolf packs" and discuss their answers to the following questions.

- *How do you think Sammy felt when other animals did not want to go near him?*
- *What do you think Dakota could do to be a friend to Skunk?*

Next, have each wolf pack share their ideas with the entire class. Then continue the story by saying, Let's find out what Dakota decided to do.

The next day I found a piece of cloth and wrapped it around my entire nose. The true test was to see if I could smell the fish I caught the day before. It passed the test! I couldn't smell anything. So I decided to go find Sammy and apologize. I found Sammy by the river all alone, as usual. I approached him carefully so I wouldn't scare him, because I knew what that meant! I sat down next to him and asked, "I didn't mean what I said earlier about you getting away, I came by to see if you wanted to do something together."

Sammy lifted his head up and said, "Sure, but what is that funny thing doing on your nose?" I told him why and then realized that Sammy didn't smell bad like he did the day before. Sammy explained that he only smells when he sprays and he only sprays if he senses danger.

"By the way," Sammy said, "remember yesterday when I sprayed that terrible odor? Well, I found out that hunters were close by and I may have saved your life!"

From that day on Sammy and I became good friends and the river became one of our favorite places to play. One day when I was on my way to meet Sammy I smelled that awful smell again and remembered what it meant so I hid. Just then a very big grizzly bear came crashing through the woods. I couldn't wait to thank my friend for saving me again from a possible dangerous situation. I decided to keep a piece of cloth tied around a branch near my den so I would always have it handy just in case!

Follow-up Questions

- Have others ever teased you about being different? How did that feel?
- What do you think are the reasons some people are mean towards others who are different from them?

Follow-up Role-Play

Role-play the following situation and then answer the questions that follow.

Characters

- A student who is deaf (uses sign language to communicate)
- A student who is afraid to be around him/her
- A student who wants to learn sign language because it's cool

Situation

The scene takes place in the cafeteria where two students are having lunch and talking to each other. The student who is deaf sits down at their table and tries to be part of the conversation. When the students notice him/her using hand signals to communicate they each start talking louder to him/her. The deaf student shakes his/her head and uses hand signals again. One of the students turns away from him/her and starts talking to another student. The other person decides to get out a piece of paper and a pencil and in writing asks the deaf student to write down what he/she said. Stop the skit.

Discuss:

- What was happening in the skit?
- What was the reason the one student decided to turn away?
- How do you think the deaf student felt when he/she did that?
- How did the other student, who wrote the note, deal with the situation?
- What would you do in this situation?

Optional Activity:

Have students act out these responses.

ACTIVITY: 3

Unscramble the words on the right and draw a line to the correct animal to show what each animal uses to protect themselves.

Animal	*How They Protect Themselves*
Skunk	____________________ ckik
Deer	____________________ yrpas
Turtle	____________________ wacls
Cat	____________________ kabe
Bird	____________________ lehsl

Dakota Meets Grinner, the Flying Squirrel*

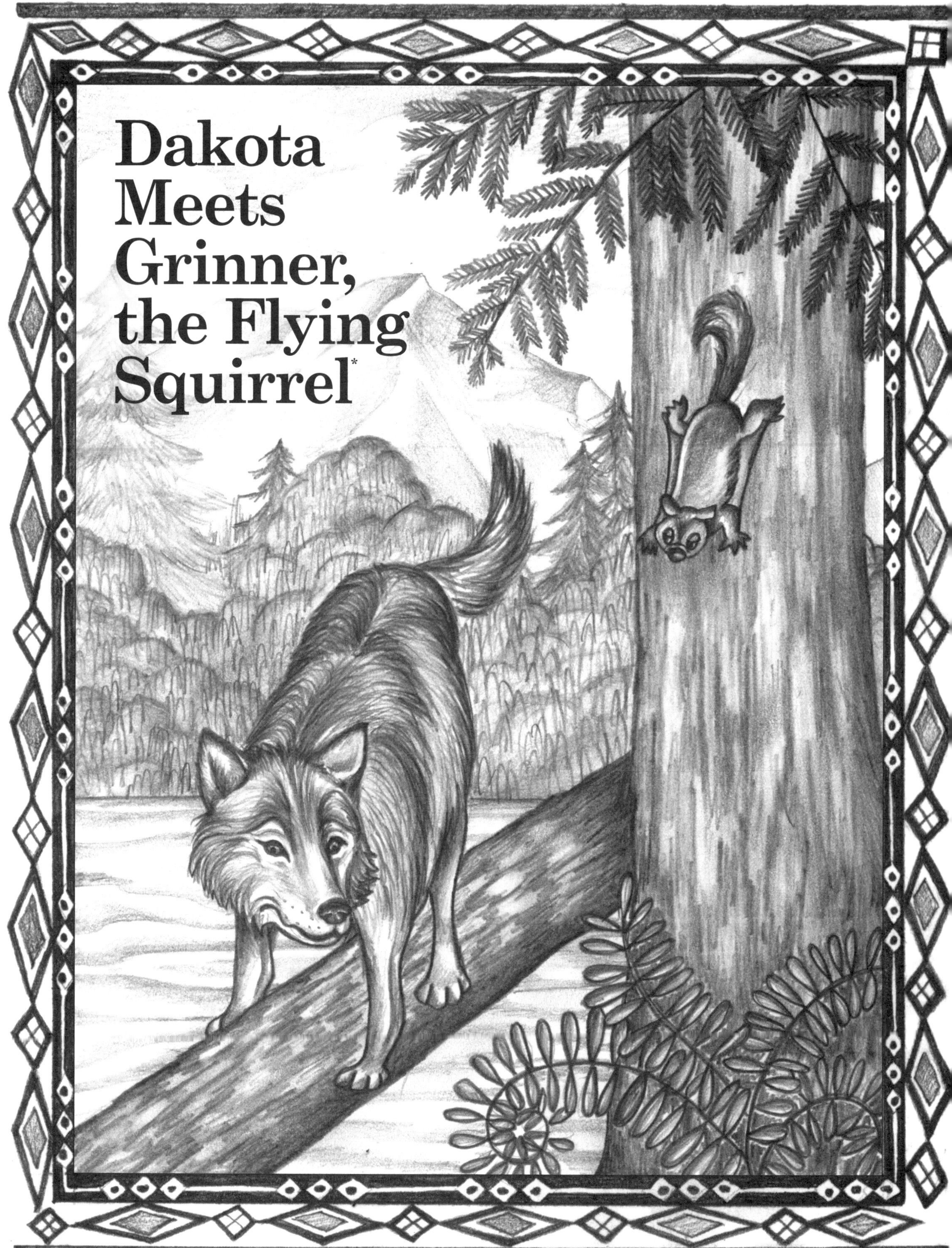

One day I was down at the river when I noticed a tree that had recently been struck by lightning. It had fallen down right over the river and made a place to cross. I decided that I would try to cross over the fallen tree even though the river seemed so far below. Well, as I walked out onto the fallen tree I made a mistake and looked down and became frightened. I froze and couldn't move! "Why was I so scared to cross, wolves are supposed to do things like this," I thought to myself. My legs started shaking and I slipped, luckily I didn't fall far from the bank of the river.

I felt very discouraged and told myself that I was a failure. I moped through the forest with my head hanging down until, suddenly I heard a sound from high up in a tree. It was a squirrel, a flying squirrel to be exact. The squirrel, gliding down from the tree, almost knocked into me and then landed right in front of where I was standing. "Hi my name is Grinner and I can understand just how you feel." He began to tell me, "I felt like a failure once when I couldn't fly like the other flying squirrels and remember how I kept telling myself, I can't, I can't!"

I asked him, "Well, how did you finally learn how to fly?" Grinner told me how he met a raccoon that showed him the secret to becoming a winner. I wondered if Grinner would share that secret with me. Grinner then stood proudly and said, "the four steps you need to learn are;

Step 1: I can be a winner.

He said, you need to believe that you can do it by realizing your personal strengths.

Step 2: I can show I'm a winner.

This is when you show through your body language that you are a winner.

Step 3: I can start like a winner.

This is when you start something with a positive, winning attitude.

Step 4: I can finish like a winner.

This is when you finish something with your best attitude."

Grinner coached me through each of the steps one at a time and then asked how I could use these steps to help me cross the fallen tree over the river.

**The 4 Step Model to being a winner and the character, Grinner, was adapted from Peer Pals by Bowman & Chanaka, AGS Publishing.*

Paws Time

Ask students to meet in their "wolf packs" and discuss their answers to the following questions.

- *How did Dakota feel when he was trying to cross the stream?*
- *How did Grinner the flying squirrel help him?*

Next, have each wolf pack share their ideas with the entire class. Then continue the story by saying, Let's find out what Dakota decided to do.

Grinner taught me that having a winning attitude is very important no matter what you do. I kept repeating the four steps and then went back to the fallen tree and stood at the edge. This time I didn't look down but told myself that I could do it. Next, I held my head high and said "I'm going to start like a winner" and took a small step and then another and another. After I took the last step and was standing on the other side I looked back and there was Grinner standing on the other side shouting, "You're a Winner!"

I finished like a winner and stood proudly on the other side of the river. I thanked Grinner for his help and realized that a positive winning attitude can help me in any situation I may be facing. Now I can prance right over that fallen tree with confidence and with my head held high!

Follow-up Questions

- Have you ever felt like you couldn't do something no matter how hard you tried?
- Share about a time you were afraid to do something.

Follow-up Role-Play

Role-play the following situation and then answer the questions that follow.

Characters

- First student who is trying to behave in class so he/she can get a "Got Ya" card (reward for behaving well in class)
- Second student who keeps getting the first student to talk out in class
- A student in class who knows the 4 steps to being a winner
- Teacher

Situation

The scene takes place in a classroom. A student is sitting in front of the class and before class begins says, "I hope I get a 'Got Ya' card today!" Another student is sitting behind him/her and keeps trying hard to get the first student's attention. The teacher reminds students that if they behave they will get a "Got Ya" card. The student sitting behind the first student ignores the teacher and keeps trying to get that student's attention. Another student who is sitting across from the first student holds up a poster that has the "4 Steps to Being A Winner" written out in bold letters. The first student whispers them to him/herself and then sits up straight and keeps looking ahead. The teacher then hands this student a "Got Ya" card and says, "This is for having a winning attitude!"

Then the teacher tells the second student that he/she has a warning for talking. Stop the skit.

Discuss:

- What was happening in the skit?
- What was the reason the second student kept trying to get the first student's attention?
- How would you handle a situation like this?

Optional Activity:

Have students act out these responses.

ACTIVITY: 4

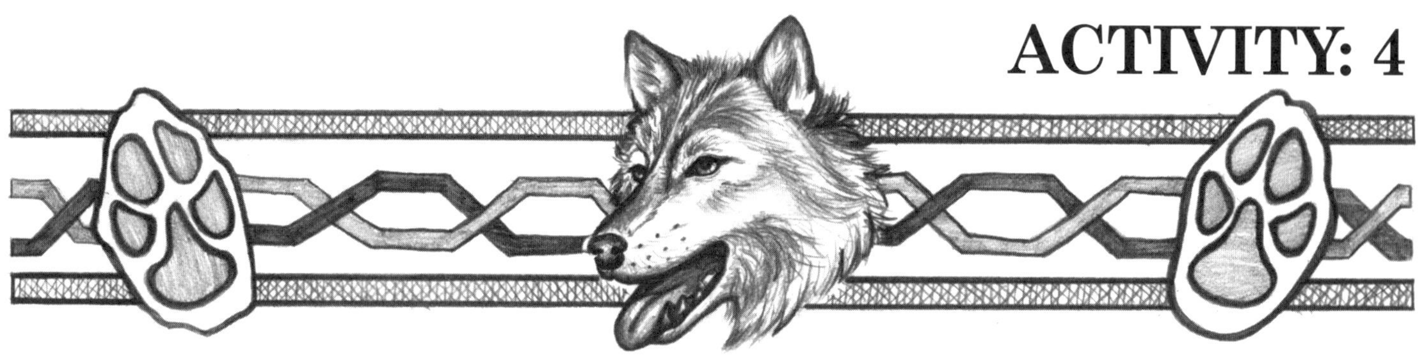

Cut out the star below.
Then write or draw something you can do well in the center.

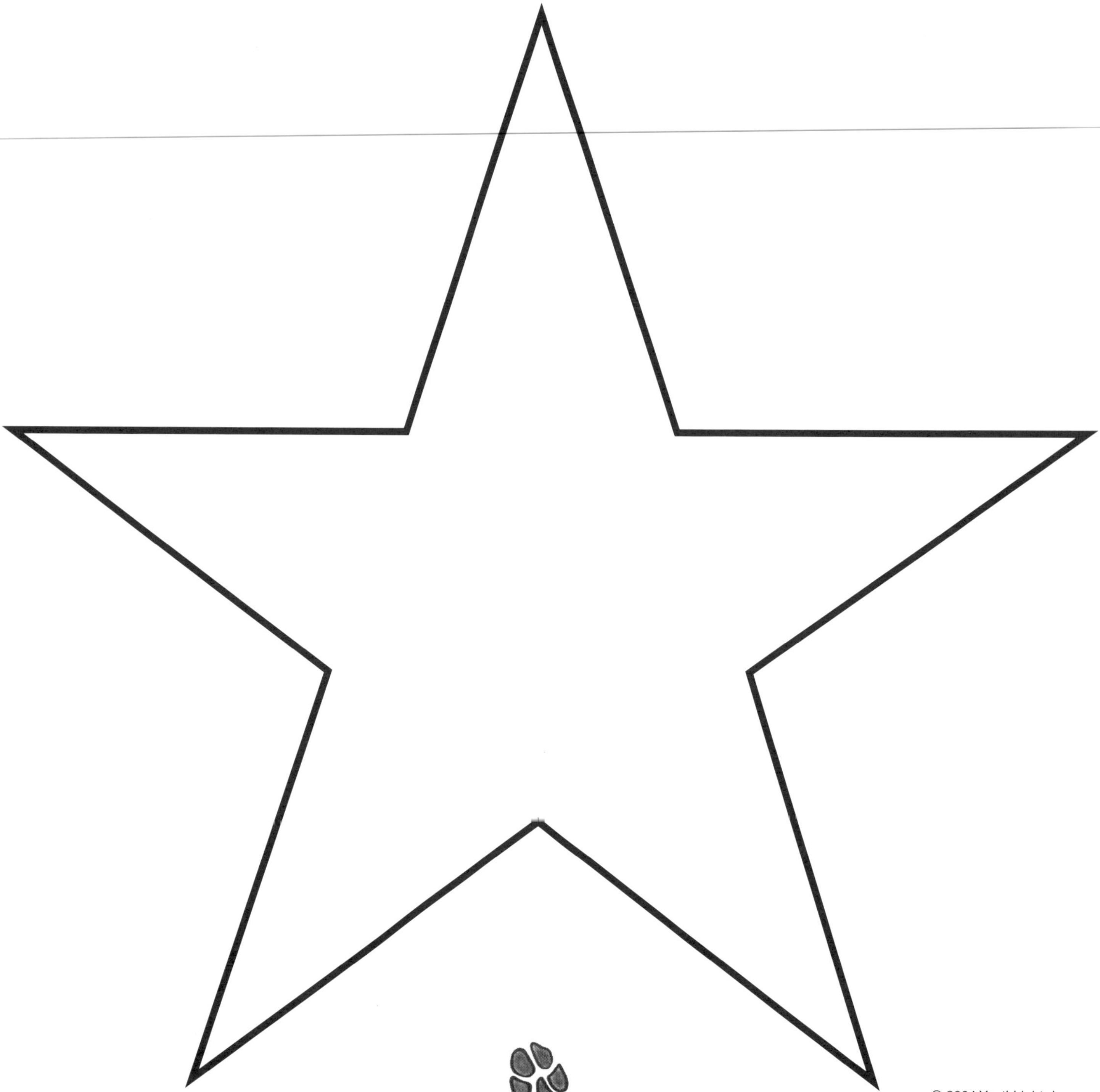

Dakota Loses His
Best Friend

Nakoma and I were always competing to see who could run the fastest, climb the highest hill in our forest, or cross the swift moving river first without falling in! It was a fun game we would play when we weren't hunting together or playing with the rest of the pack. One day I said to Nakoma, "I'll beat you to the top of "Rocky Point!" (a rocky ledge that overlooked the valley below) I shouted, "Ready, Set, Go!" and we both ran as fast as we could toward Rocky Point.

All of a sudden Nakoma slipped on some loose rocks and tumbled head over heals down the side of the ledge. I watched helplessly and then quickly ran down to see if he was okay. Nakoma could not stand up at first but then slowly pulled himself up, shook himself off and was able to limp back home with me at his side to support him.

Once we were home, the other wolves took turns licking Nakoma's wounds. Our mom insisted he go to "Luca", an older wolf who knew how to care for the injured or sick. She lived on the other side of the forest. Nakoma, being the free-spirited and stubborn wolf that he was would not go. He said, "I'm not hurt that bad and ... I can take care of myself!"

We were all worried about my brother and I offered to go with him to Luca's. Two days passed and Nakoma didn't look any better. He finally admitted he needed the old wolf's help and said he was going to go to Luca's den first thing in the morning.

When morning came I didn't see Nakoma so I decided to follow his scent. It led me down a winding path. I noticed something lying on the ground ahead. It was Nakoma. He wasn't moving! I barked at Nakoma to get up, but he didn't move. I didn't want to believe he was dead and kept nudging him with my nose. I was trying to wake him up. Then I realized he wasn't going to get up, ever. I was very sad and ran back to tell my parents and the rest of the pack. They followed me back to where Nakoma was lying.

After sniffing and nudging Nakoma, we all looked up at the sky and howled together to express our sadness. I believe that our howls could be heard across the horizon that day.

I remember feeling so many different emotions. I felt bad that I was the one who got Nakoma to race up to Rocky Point, and angry that Nakoma refused to get help right away when he needed it. I couldn't believe this was happening to me. How could I possibly go on without my brother, my best friend? It was as if there was a hole in my heart. What could I do to get through this difficult time?

Paws Time

Ask students to meet in their "wolf packs" and discuss their answers to the following questions.

- *How do you think Dakota felt when Nakoma wouldn't go for help?*
- *What could Dakota do to help him with the loss of his brother?*

Next, have each wolf pack share their ideas with the entire class. Then continue the story by saying, "Let's find out what Dakota decided to do."

This was a very sad time not just for me but for the entire pack. The pack was very helpful in listening to my feelings. The sad feelings continued for a while until they came just every now and then. I tried to focus more on the good memories I had with Nakoma.

I decided to go visit all those special places where we used to go together. While I sat at each place I remembered the special times together with Nakoma. I made a special spot to always remind me of Nakoma and our special times together. I placed some rocks in a mound and packed it with mud so it wouldn't fall down. Sometimes I would go to that spot and pretend Nakoma was there and tell him about my day. After some time I no longer went there alone but brought another member of the pack (Jesse) with me. Soon I could have fun again spending time with Jesse and making new memories with my special friend.

Follow-up Questions

- What is it like when a pet, a friend, a parent or other special person dies?
- When have you experienced a loss of a pet or a special person?
- What is one thing you can do to help someone or yourself get through a difficult time such as having someone or something close to you die?

Follow-up Role-Play

Role-play the following situation and then answer the questions that follow.

Characters

- A student who lost his/her pet dog
- A friend of the student who tries to comfort him/her
- A student who says something mean

Situation

A student is crying because he/she had to put their dog to sleep the day before and they were very close. The student is sharing about how difficult it was to say goodbye forever. The friend of the student is trying to comfort him/her when another student walks over and says something like, "It was just a dog!" Stop the skit.

Discuss:

- What was happening in the skit?
- How do you think the student who lost his/her dog was feeling?
- What do you think was the reason for that student's uncaring comment?
- How could the student who was feeling sad respond to the other student's comment?

Optional Activity:

Have students act out these responses.

ACTIVITY: 5

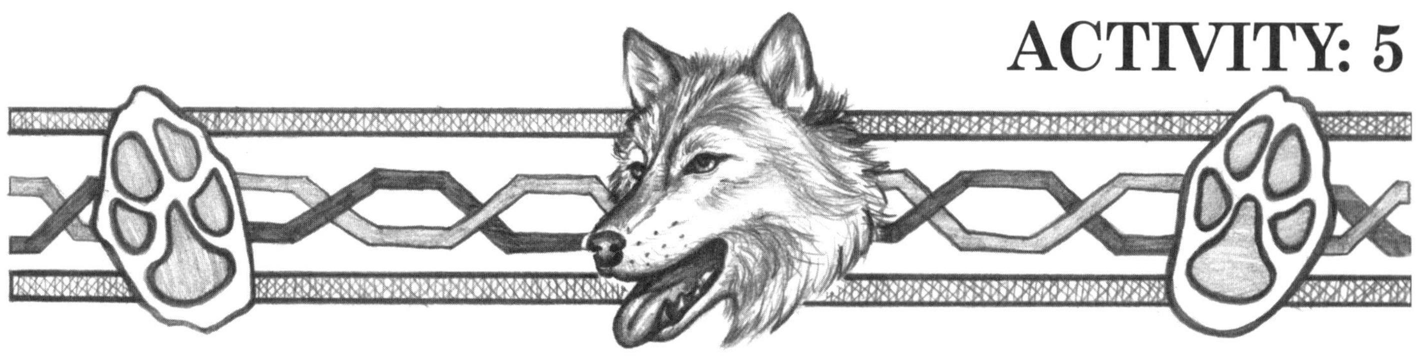

In the picture frame, draw a person, pet or thing that you lost.
Then, draw a happy memory in each cloud.

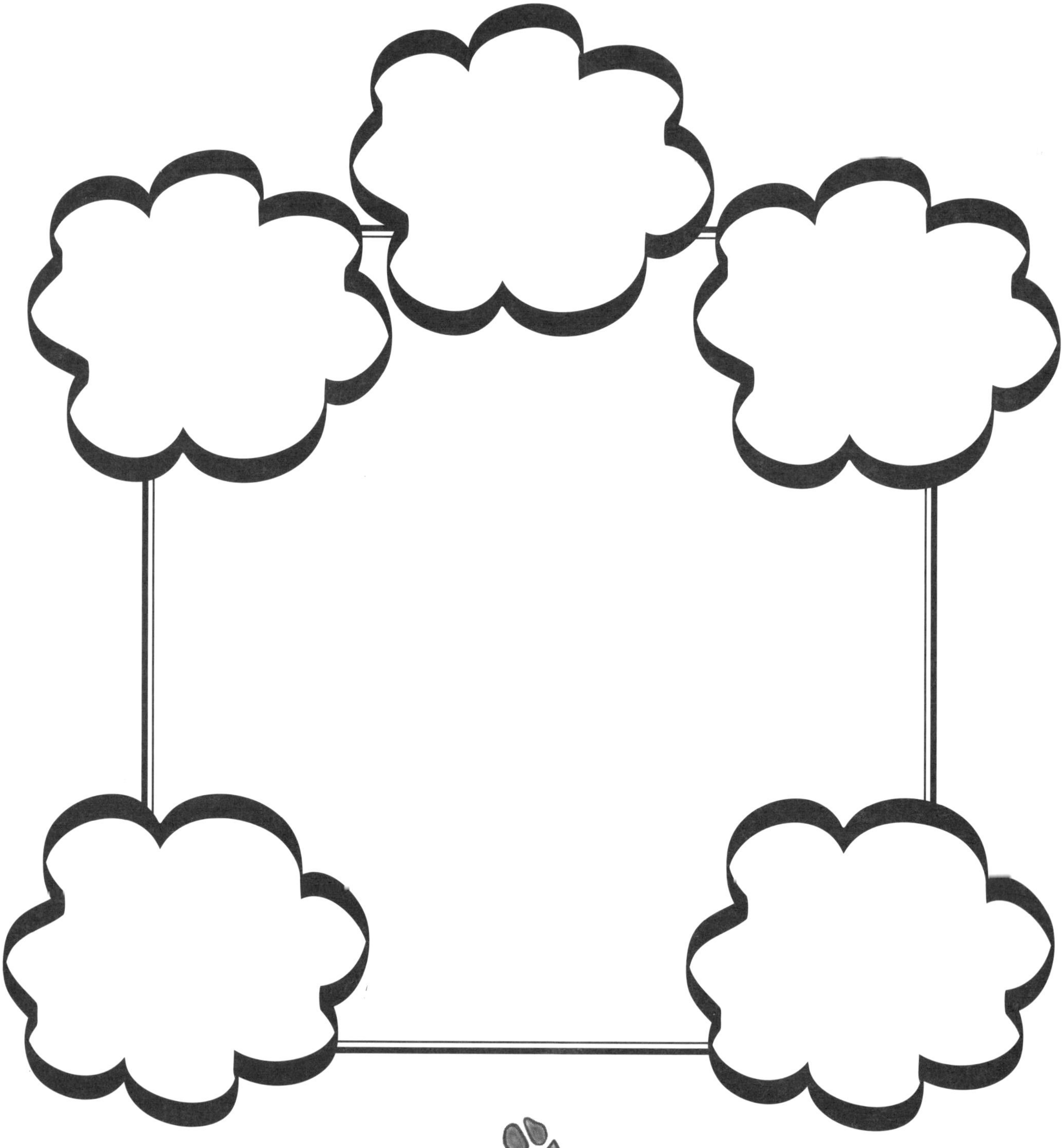

Dakota and "Badge"
the Angry Badger

One day, I decided to go to my favorite lookout spot by the river. I wanted to relax and watch the salmon as they swam upstream through the fast water in the rapids. I enjoyed watching how the bears would catch the salmon as they flipped wildly out of the water. I figured that I might learn some tips that would help me to catch a few fish of my own. And I loved eating fish, bones and all! But, to my surprise, as I came closer to my favorite spot I noticed that another animal was laying and relaxing right there in my special spot by the stream! As I walked closer to see who this intruder was, I suddenly stopped when I noticed it was Badge, the angry badger.

Badge snarled, "Get away from here!"

I barked back, "this is my favorite place, what do you think you are doing here?"

Badge threatened, "I don't see your name on this rock that I'm sitting on. You don't own it. So get lost or you'll be sorry."

The bears were irritated to hear all this arguing. They decided they were going further downstream to fish. I didn't know how to respond to Badge because I knew how mean and dangerous he could become when he was angry. But after I thought about it for while, I started becoming angry myself. I just couldn't get it out of my head that Badge had stolen my favorite spot. So I snarled back, "Well, I don't see your name on the rock either!"

Now my heart was beating very fast and loud. My ears and the fur on my back stood straight up. This made me feel very uncomfortable. I knew that Badge was known to be one of the most mean and dangerous fighters — especially if he didn't get his own way. I thought to myself, "How can I get Badge off my rock?"

Paws Time

Ask students to meet in their "wolf packs" and discuss their answers to the following questions.

- *How do you think Badge felt when Dakota told him that this was his special spot?*
- *What could Dakota do in this situation?*

Next, have each wolf pack share their ideas with the entire class. Then continue the story by saying, "Let's find out what Dakota decided to do."

I found an open field nearby and started running as fast as I could. Running sometimes helped me think more clearly. I was so furious and felt like fighting Badge, but I knew I would probably get hurt. Also, fighting might get us both in trouble. Besides, fighting would only prove to Badge that there was no other way to work out our differences.

I decided to talk to the male leader of our pack, Kewanee, the Alpha male. After hearing my story he replied, "Since Badge didn't realize that this was your special spot, It wasn't fair for you to tell Badge to move. He has just as much right to be there as you do. So if you still want to use this spot you need to work out a way that you both can use it."

I knew he was right but how was I going to communicate this to Badge? I decided to visit Badge. I found him in the same spot and calmly said, "Badge, I'm sorry for what I said earlier. I know this isn't my spot but I do like to come here sometimes. Can we work out a way to both use this spot and not get so mad at each other?"

At first Badge wouldn't even look at me. But then to my surprise he turned toward me and said, "Well, alright, I guess we can both use the rock but, what would other animals think, a wolf and a badger sitting on the same rock, beside each other. I have a reputation to keep and don't want other animals to think I'm turning too nice!"

"Don't worry It will be our little secret," I whispered back. Then we both starting laughing so hard we rolled off the rock and right into the river. We both learned a valuable lesson that day. "Laughing is a lot more fun than being angry…even if it gets you all wet!"

Follow-up Questions

- Have you ever been really mad because someone did something that you didn't think was fair to you?
- What did you do about it? What was the outcome?

Follow-up Role-Play

Role-play the following situation and then answer the questions that follow.

Characters

- A student who does not want to share with other students
- 2-3 students who get angry at the student for not sharing
- A third student who says they are going to go tell the teacher

Situation

During Art class students are taking turns with some art supplies. One student decided he/she does not want to share with the other students. Several other students get angry and threaten the student. Another student says that he/she is going to tell the teacher if they don't share with them. Stop the skit.

Discuss:

- What was happening in the skit?
- How were the students trying to get the one student to share?
- What do you think will happen?
- What would you do to get that student to share?

Optional Activity:

Have students act out these responses.

ACTIVITY: 6

Put a ♡ next to the things you should share with others and an ✘ next to things you shouldn't share.

______ Hairbrush 

______ Crayons 

______ Books 

______ Toys 

______ A drink 

______ A sunset 

______ A seesaw 

______ An ice cream cone 

Dakota Meets "Nikki"
the Wolfdog

It was an early spring after a very cold, snowy winter. I couldn't wait to explore the beauty of the forest with its' colorful flowers and blossoming trees. As I ran up to the top of Rocky Point I could see a perfect view of the whole forest. It was so beautiful that for a moment I thought about how Nakoma would have enjoyed seeing it too. All of a sudden, I saw something quickly running through the field of wildflowers below. Curious about what this new creature could be, I ran down the rocky point to investigate. As I got closer it was gone, or so I thought.

Suddenly, the mysterious creature came running past me and I yelled, "Hey Wait!" Startled, the animal stopped and we both stood there staring at each other.

I wasn't sure if this animal I was looking at was a wolf or a dog so I sniffed her and asked, "Hey, I'm Dakota a wolf, Uh, who, what are you?"

She replied, "I'm Nikki, my dad is a wolf, but my mother is a dog."

"So does that mean that you are a wolf dog," I questioned.

"Many animals make fun of me because I'm mixed and call me a mutt or half-breed," she explained.

I told Nikki that I wasn't like those animals that said mean things to her. "I remember being picked on just because I was a wolf," I told her.

Nikki didn't know what she could do to make the other animals stop calling her names. "I want them to realize that even though I may look different from other wolves, I am just like them in many other ways." Nikki looked up at me and continued, "What do you think I could do to show the other animals that?

Paws Time

Ask students to meet in their "wolf packs" and discuss their answers to the following questions.

- *If you could speak animal what would you say to those animals about Nikki?*
- *How can Nikki convince the other animals that she is just like them?*

Next, have each wolf pack share their ideas with the entire class. Then continue the story by saying, "Let's find out what Nikki and Dakota decided to do."

Nikki and I decided to meet and play together quite often. I introduced Nikki to the other wolves in our pack and before long Nikki had a new set of friends. Some of the other animals that used to pick on Nikki got to know her better and discovered that she was really nice. The other wolves accepted her into the pack so Nikki not only had a new group of friends but she now had others who would help her if she ever needed it. I learned that to accept others we need to look much deeper than the outside appearance.

Follow-up Questions

- Is there someone you know who has parents very different from each other, for example parents of two different nationalities?
- Have you ever felt like Nikki or knew someone who did? What happened?
- How do you think people can accept all races and nationalities?

Follow-up Role-Play

Role-play the following situation and then answer the questions that follow.

Characters

- A student who was adopted from another country
- Two students who ask questions about why the other student looks different from his/her parents

Situation

Three students are working together on a group project. One student in the group is of a different cultural background than the other two. The other two students start asking questions about where he/she is from and why he/she looks different than his/her parents. The adopted student starts to feel confused about all the questions and wonders why he/she is so different.
Stop the skit.

Discuss:

- What was happening in the skit?
- How did the students feel about the adopted student?
- Were the questions to the adopted student helpful?
- What could they have done or said that would have caused the adopted student to feel accepted?

Optional Activity:

Have students act out these responses.

ACTIVITY: 7

Find out some ways you are different and ways you are the same as other students in your pack. Write these below.

Different	***Same***

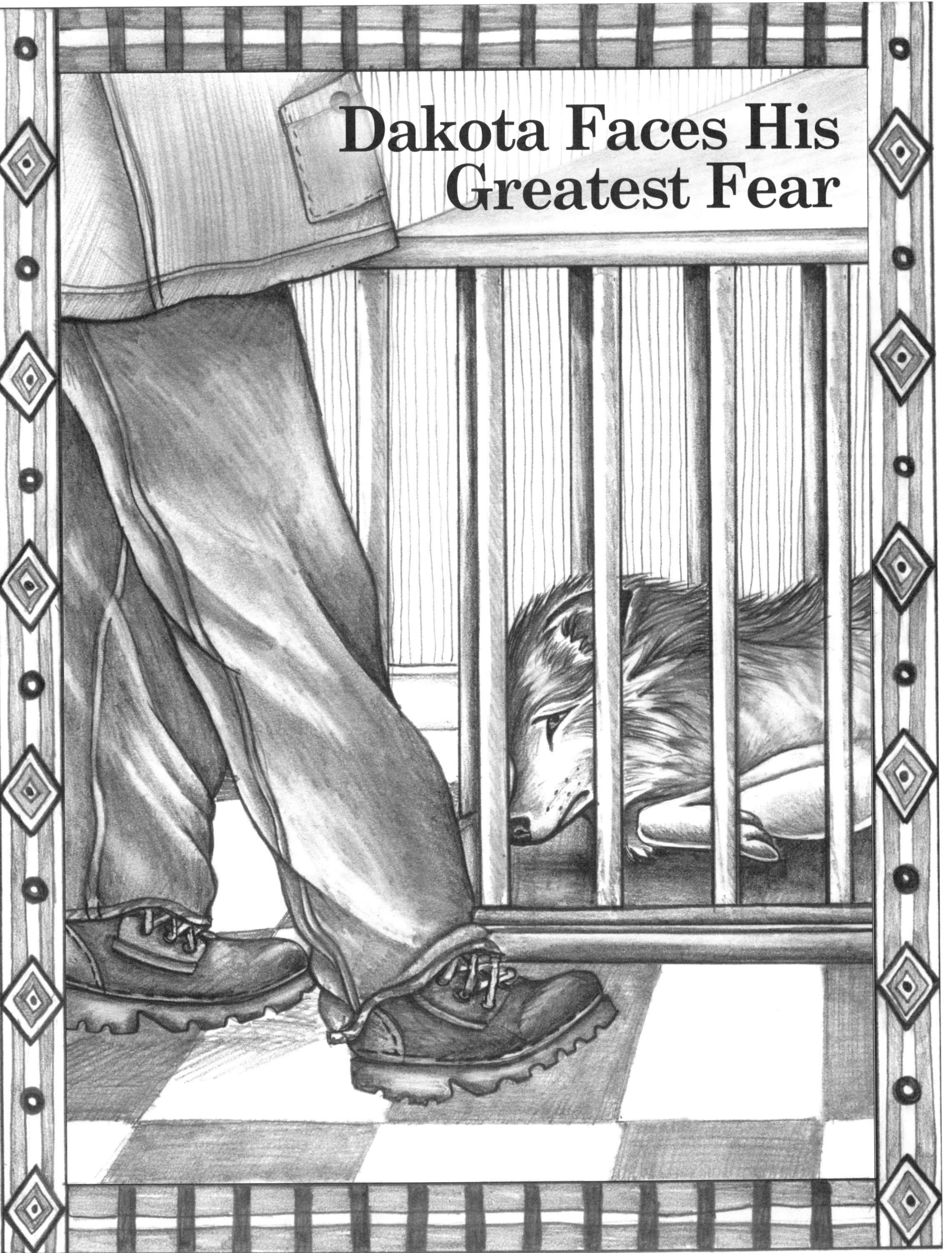
Dakota Faces His
Greatest Fear

Growing up, I always learned that a wolf's greatest fear is… humans! I heard awful stories about how many of my relatives had been either poisoned, shot at or trapped. Many times it was because humans could get lots of money for wolf fur. Sometimes it was because they just hated wolves. So I grew up with a terrible fear of humans. But one day I had to face that fear.

I was walking along the edge of the forest one beautiful sunny day when all of a sudden, I heard something very scary. It was a clicking sound. I heard it again and then felt something hit the side of my body.

The next thing I remembered was falling down into a deep sleep and then waking up inside a strange metal box in a strange looking place. I was so scared and thought I might be killed and never see my pack again!

When I looked up, I saw four humans standing around me. At least I thought they were humans since they looked so different from animals in the forest. I was still groggy from whatever hit me but especially scared that they were going to hurt me. Then they opened the door to the box and carried me out. I realized then that I was at the place the other wolves called "The Refuge" a place where they help hurt and wounded wolves.

They put this collar-like thing around my neck and then led me back into the metal box. Then they took me back to the forest and let me go free! I slowly walked

away, back into the woods. I couldn't believe I was back in the forest and still alive! I wondered why this thing was on my neck and why they didn't hurt me. I hurried home to tell the pack about what happened.

Paws Time

Ask students to meet in their "wolf packs" and discuss their answers to the following questions.

- *What do you think was going through Dakota's mind when he woke up and saw all those people around him?*
- *How do you think Dakota felt about humans after he was released without being harmed? What do you think the collar was for?*

Next, have each wolf pack share their ideas with the entire class. Then continue the story by saying, "Let's find out what Dakota learned."

I told the pack what had happened. The Alpha wolf, Kewanee told me that he had the same experience except his collar later came off after he wore it for a few years. Puzzled, I asked, "What is it for?" Kewane explained, " it is a tracking collar to help the good humans learn where we are and to help keep our pack safe from harm." He also said that they usually look for the wolf that appears to be the pack's leader so they can follow the entire pack. I realized that I must be special to have been chosen to wear this collar.

Kewanee called a special pack meeting and told the pack that he was getting too old to lead the pack and that I would now become the new Alpha male in the pack. "Wow, me an Alpha wolf!" This was one of the most exciting days of my life. Now that I have gained respect from my pack I can teach them many of the helpful things that I have learned.

One thing I would teach them is that not all humans are mean to wolves but some actually want to help save us from other humans who don't understand us. I also learned that fear comes from what we do not understand. And what we do not understand, we fear. What a better world it would be if more humans could learn how important wolves are and how helpful wolves can be to others. Maybe all of you who listened to my stories will teach others the truth about wolves. The more people understand the truth the better our chances for survival.

Follow-up Questions

- What is your greatest fear? Where did that fear come from?
- What have you tried to do to not be afraid?

Follow-up Role-Play

Role-play the following situation and then answer the questions that follow.

Characters

- A student's first day at school
- Parent(s) of the student
- Teacher
- Several students sitting in the classroom

Situation

It is the night before the beginning of the school year. A student is afraid they will have a mean teacher because he/she heard that the teachers at this school were mean. The parents of this student say things like, "you will be fine, I'm sure your teacher will be nice." The next morning the student starts to not feel well and says he/she needs to stay home. The parent tells him/her they have to go to school. The student starts to cry. At school the student slowly walks into his/her assigned class. The teacher greets all the students with a smile and asks if any of them felt afraid before coming to school. Amazingly, several students raised their hands! Stop the skit.

Discuss:

- What was happening in the skit?
- How many of you ever felt like this?
- What caused the student to be afraid?
- What helped her/him to not be afraid?

Optional Activity:

Have students act out these responses.

ACTIVITY: 8

Answer the following questions about fears.

1. **What would you tell someone who is afraid of the dark?**

2. **Circle where you feel afraid.**

   Head *Stomach* *Hands* *Legs* *Chest* *Throat*

3. **What is your greatest fear?**

   Dark *Strangers* *Failing a Test* *War* *School*

   Losing a Loved One *Being Bullied* *Other*__________________

4. **Who can you talk to about your fears?**

   Parent(s) *School Counselor* *Teacher* *Friend* *Pet*

   *Other*________________________

5. **Draw a fear you used to have but don't any more.**

Dakota's Goodbye

I hope you enjoyed sharing in some of my adventures. I hope you also learned some lessons to help you in your own personal life. I bet you never thought you could learn from a wolf! I want to encourage you to find out as much information as you can about wolves and have included a section called "Wolf Facts." This section will help you understand what wolves have faced throughout the years and what efforts have been taken to increase survival. I will also provide some web sites that you and a parent can go to for more information about wolves and what people are doing across the nation to help. Some of these web sites include activities and pictures.

Thank you for being part of this program. You have all earned the title of "Alpha Wolf" and have earned a special certificate to show you have completed the program. Whenever you work in groups again, think of your wolf packs and how you worked together to make decisions. Remember to always listen to each other's ideas and use your personal strengths to find solutions to life's challenges.

Thanks for your interest in us wolves! Please spread the word to others about what we are really like and maybe one day we won't have to struggle to survive but live in peace. ***"OWWWWWOO!"***

Your friend,

Dakota

Congratulations!

The person who's name is listed on this certificate is awarded the

Alpha Award

for successfully completing Dakota's program.

Student's Name

Student's School

Program Leader

Some Wolf Facts[*]

Wolves are some of the most intelligent and devoted of all creatures. So how did they get such a bad reputation? When European settlers first came to North America they killed millions of buffalo. Buffalo being the main food source for the wolves were nearly exterminated and the wolves were forced to eat livestock that were now grazing in the buffalo's place. Farmers and ranchers shot, poisoned, burned and trapped the wolves to keep them away from their livestock. Hunters and trappers joined the terrible attack against the wolves. Their goal was to kill every wolf in sight. It has been estimated that over a million wolves lost their lives. These farmers and ranchers told very negative stories about wolves to their children and their children's children and these are still heard to this day.

Although there is no record of a man, woman or child being attacked by a healthy wolf in the wild, still, many people continue to hate wolves. Some people wanted to bring the wolves back into the national parks but went about it the wrong way. They captured over thirty wolves from Canada, put them in crates and brought them back to the US. Many angry people tried to stop them and by doing so the wolves were left in their small crates for weeks. Once the wolves were finally set free they were forced to live in new surroundings where they were not welcomed but hated by ranchers and farmers who never wanted them there in the first place. Many wolves were separated from their families to come back to the states and the sad thing is no one ever considered how they felt about moving.

Wolf killings are still going on today by mostly farmers and ranchers who do not agree with the wolves returning. Many organizations are trying to change their mind about the wolves by purchasing guard dogs, hiring cowboys to watch over the herds and replacing any livestock lost due to a wolf attack. These programs are very costly and can not possibly stop all the attacks on wolves. Some wolves are being sold as pets and because of their wild nature, the owners end up being abusive or neglectful to them.

Wolf sanctuaries exist across the country to care for abused, wounded or abandoned wolves and their pups. Some are returned to the wild and radio collars are used to help keep track of their progress. Many sanctuaries care for the wolves for life because so many can no longer survive in the wild. Wolves need your help. You can help by finding out what is going on in your own state and learning the truth about wolves.

[*] *Information on facts was obtained from the following web sites;*

www.wolveswolveswolves.org/MythsAndLies.htm
www.Wolfsource.org
www.defenders.org
www.wolfsanctuary.com

The Maligned Wolf

The forest was my home. I lived there, and I cared about it. I tried to keep it neat and clean.

Then one sunny day, while I was cleaning up some garbage a camper had left behind, I heard footsteps. I leaped behind a tree and saw a little girl coming down the trail carrying a basket. I was suspicious of this little girl right away because she was dressed funny-all in red, and her head was covered up as if she didn't want people to know who she was. Naturally, I stopped to check her out. I asked who she was, where she was going, where she had come from, and all of that. She gave me a "song and dance" about going to her grandmother's house with a basket of lunch. She appeared to be a basically honest person, but she was in my forest, and she certainly looked suspicious with that strange get up of hers. So I decided to teach her just how serious it is to prance through the forest unannounced and dressed funny.

I let her go on her way, but I ran ahead to her grandmother's house. When I saw that nice old woman, I explained my problem and she agreed that her granddaughter needed to learn a lesson all right. The old woman agreed to stay out of sight until I called her. Actually, she hid under the bed.

When the girl arrived, I invited her into the bedroom where I was in the bed, dressed like the grandmother. The girl came in all rosy-cheeked and said something nasty about my big ears. I've been insulted before so I made the best of it by suggesting that big ears would help me to hear better.

Now, what I meant was that I liked her and wanted to pay close attention to what she was saying. But she made another insulting crack about my bulging eyes. Now you can see how I was beginning to feel about this girl who put on such a nice front, but was apparently a very nasty person. Still, I've made it a policy to turn the other cheek, so I told her that my big eyes helped me to see her better.

Her next insult really got to me. I've got this problem with having big teeth, and that little girl made an insulting crack about them. I know that I should have had better control, but I leaped up form the bed and growled that my teeth would help me to eat her better.

Now let's face it – no wolf could ever eat a little girl – everyone knows that – but that crazy girl started running around the house screaming – me chasing her to calm her down. I'd taken off the grandmother clothes, but that only seemed to make it worse. All of a sudden the door came crashing open, and a big lumberjack was standing there with his axe. I looked at him, and all of a sudden it came clear that I was in trouble. There was an open window behind me, and out I went.

I'd like to say that was the end of it. But that grandmother character never did tell my side of the story. Before long the word got around that I was a mean, nasty guy. Everybody started avoiding me. I don't know about that little girl with the funny red outfit, but I did not live happily ever after.

Author Unknown

APPENDIX: C

Information About Wolves and Wolf Recovery

Web Sites for more information on wolf recovery programs:

www.wolfsanctuary.com

www.nawa.org

www.wolveswolveswolves.org

www.defenders.org

www.savewolves.org

www.savealaskawolves.org

www.boomerwolf.com

www.wolf.org

List of recommended books and activities for kids:

www.kidsplanet.org

www.wolfsource.org/books.html

www.nwf.org/kids

www.wolfweb.com/books

www.education.eku.edu

www.nawa.org/educational

www.discoverykids.com

Additional Classroom Activities

1. Discuss with the class how billboards carry important messages through using pictures or symbols. What are some billboards they remember seeing? What was the message? Create a billboard about your favorite animal.

2. Have students select an animal they are interested in. Have them research their animal using information from the library and on the internet. Then, have the students share this information by:

   - writing a paragraph.
   - drawing pictures of what their animal looks like.
   - making a collage using pictures from magazines.

3. Bring in wildlife professionals to speak to the class about different wild animals, their habitat and what threatens them. Many times these people can bring some wild animals with them. Your local Department of Wildlife should be able to help you.

4. Purchase the "Healing Species" curriculum for your school. Or, have a "Healing Species Instructor" come to your school to conduct their 11 week curriculum using rescued dogs. *(For more information on this program contact Cheri Brown Thompson at 803-535-6543 or YouthLight, Inc. at 800-209-9774)*

5. Hold a school-wide "Call of the Wild" week and have contests for each grade level on:
   - the best animal drawing.
   - the best design for a wildlife stamp.
   - the best photo taken of wildlife.
   - the best wildlife project.
   - the best invention to help wildlife.
   - the best animal model.
   - the best act of kindness toward wildlife.

6. Take a class trip to a wildlife park, zoo or wildlife sanctuary.

7. Hold a "Pet Day" for your class. Have students bring in photos of their favorite pet. (if they do not have a pet, they can talk about a pet they know) Each student can share something amazing or special that this pet can do.

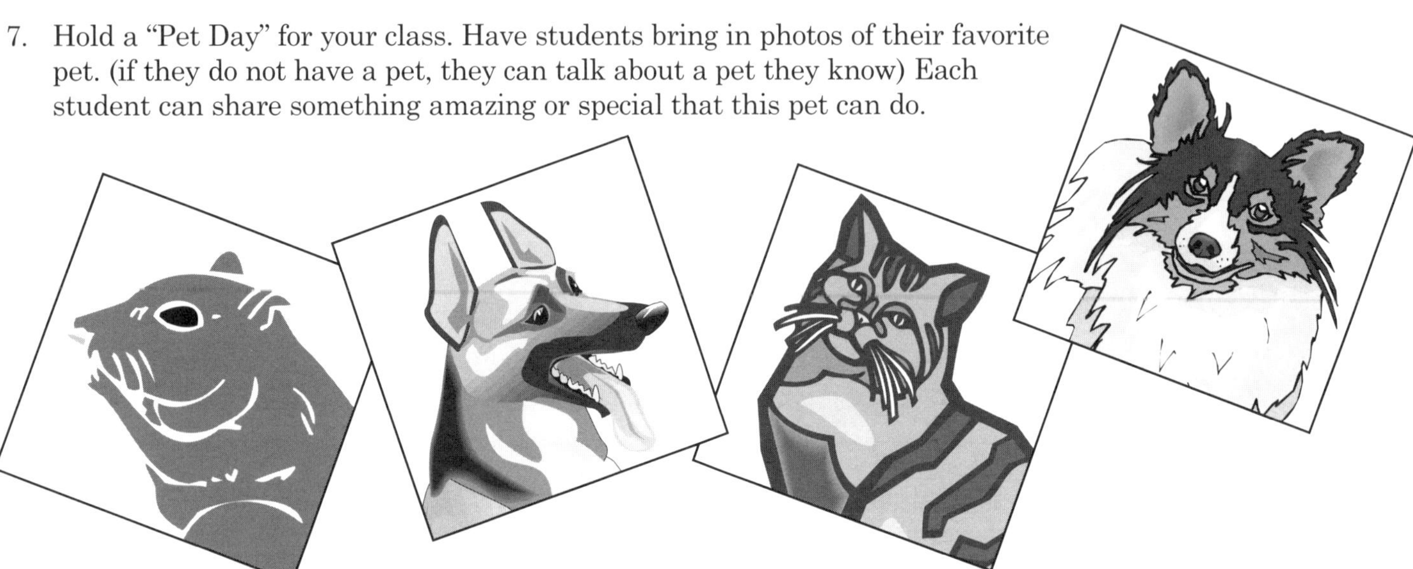

8. Show an episode of "Miracle Pets" or other TV program that shows how animals have saved people's lives. Have a class discussion about how devoted pets are and their willingness to risk their life to save a person.

9. Have your class "Adopt a Pet" from a local animal shelter to care for. Allow students to brainstorm ways to raise money to feed and care for their pet and to help find the pet a good home. The students can also visit the pet on weekends with their parent(s).

10. Have a classroom pet that student can take turns caring for. Students can sign up for their day to feed and care for the pet. With parents permission some students may be able to take the pet home during holidays and school closings. (possible pets may include; hamster, guinea pig, mouse, gerbil, rabbit, snake or lizard)